TRAPDOOR SPIDERS

THE SPIDER DISCOVERY LIBRARY

Louise Martin

Rourke Enterprises, Inc.
Vero Beach, Florida 32964

LIBRARY OF CONGRESS
Library of Congress Cataloging-in-Publication Data

Martin, Louise, 1955-
 Trapdoor spiders/by Louise Martin.

 p. cm. — (The Spider discovery library)
 Includes index.
 Summary: Describes the physical characteristics, habits,
and natural environment of the large, hairy spiders that
build hinged trapdoors at the entrance of their burrows.
 ISBN 0-86592-963-7
 1. Trap-door spiders — Juvenile literature. [1. Trap-door
spiders. 2. Spiders.] I. Title. II Series:
Martin, Louise, 1955-
Spider discovery library.
QL458.4.M36   1988   88-5968
595.4'4 - dc19   CIP
                           AC

Printed in the USA

*Title page photo: A trapdoor spider
in the defensive posture*

TABLE OF CONTENTS

TRAPDOOR SPIDERS

Trapdoor spiders belong to a group of spiders known as *Mygalomorphs.* This group includes many of the very large, hairy spiders. Trapdoor spiders get their name from the hinged trapdoors they build at the entrance to their burrows. The trapdoors hide the holes in the ground that lead into the burrows where the spiders live. They help to make the spiders' homes safe from **predators**.

A trapdoor spider grips the door to its hole

HOW THEY LOOK

There are many different kinds of trapdoor spiders. They are found in countries all around the world. Some, like this big trapdoor spider from the family *Ummidia*, have very hairy bodies and legs. Other kinds are smaller and less hairy. Trapdoor spiders are usually brown in color. This makes them hard to spot against the brown earth.

A large, hairy trapdoor spider

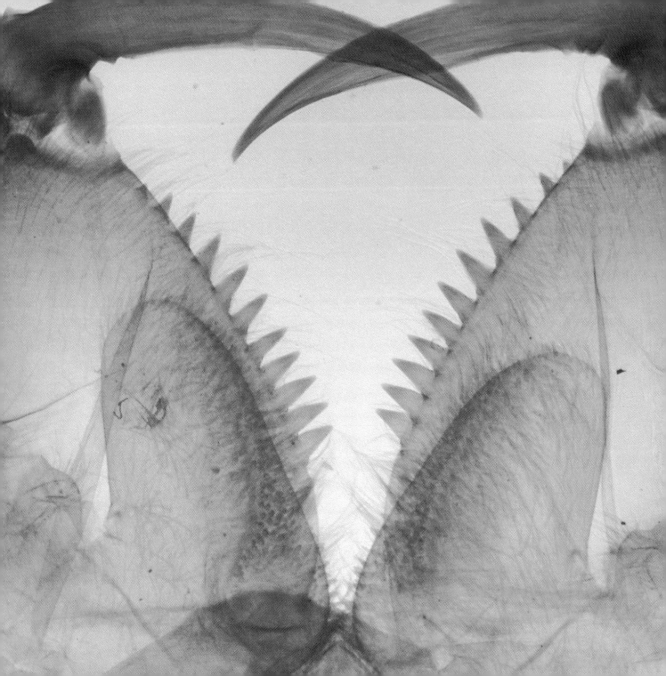

WHERE THEY LIVE

Trapdoor spiders live in burrows dug in the ground. They use rake-like spines on their fangs to dig out the earth. As the spiders dig down, they build up the walls of the burrow to make sure they don't cave in. First they use a mixture of soil and **saliva** to waterproof the walls, then they line all or part of the burrow with their silk. The burrow may be as deep as 12 inches.

Trapdoor spiders use the "rakes" on their fangs to dig burrows

SILK TRAPDOORS

When the burrow is just deep enough for the spider to crawl into, and the walls have been made safe, the spider begins to work on the trapdoor. They can build two types of doors. One is a very thin door, which the spider makes of silk. It rests gently over the opening to the burrow. When this kind of trapdoor is used, there is often a second "security" door lower down in the burrow.

Some spiders build very thin trapdoors

The hinged trapdoor fits tightly over the entrance to the burrow

A male trapdoor spider in the
defensive posture

CORK TRAPDOORS

The most common form of door is the "cork" trapdoor. It fits tightly into the mouth of the burrow, like a cork in a bottle. When in place, it is very difficult to see. The "cork" trapdoor is much thicker than the silk door. The spider makes the door from layers of earth and silk, and attaches the finished trapdoor to the entrance of the burrow with a hinge.

There may be a spider lurking just inside this burrow

THEIR BURROWS

Trapdoor spiders build different kinds of burrows. Some of the Australian **species** make burrows with two tunnels. The wishbone spider, *Dekana,* builds two entrances to its burrow so that it is shaped like an upturned wishbone. If a predator attacks down one tunnel, the spider can run out the other side. Other trapdoor spiders may build a small chamber off their single-tunneled burrows, where they can hide from predators.

Some trapdoor spiders lay tripwires like this around their burrows

HUNTING FROM BURROWS

Trapdoor spiders that build silk trapdoors have another way of catching their prey. They lie in wait down in the burrow. As soon as they hear an insect nearby, they burst out through the thin trapdoor to seize it. Some spiders build tripwires made of silk close to their trapdoors. An insect who stumbles over the silk threads becomes easy prey for the spiders.

A shiny black trapdoor spider from Western Australia

PREY

All trapdoor spiders are **nocturnal** and hunt at night. They hunt their **prey** in two main ways. Some kinds climb up the burrow to the entrance, prop open the trapdoor, and stick out their head and front two pairs of legs. The rest of their bodies stays in the hole. When they see a juicy beetle passing by, the spiders quickly pounce and drag the victim into the burrow to eat.

Trapdoor spiders live in many different countries.

THEIR DEFENSES

The trapdoor spider's main line of defense is its burrow, with its **camouflaged** trapdoor. As we have seen, the trapdoor is not easy to find. But some creatures know what to look for. If they can catch the spider unaware, they are usually in luck. They fling the door open. The spider runs to hide, perhaps through a second door further down the burrow, and is often trapped. If the spider knows it is under attack, it clings on to the underside of the door, so that the predator cannot open it.